Roger Casement
Human Rights Hero

Written by Gaye Shortland
and illustrated by Derry Dillon

IRELAND'S BEST KNOWN STORIES
IN A
NUTSHELL

Published 2016
Poolbeg Press Ltd

123 Grange Hill, Baldoyle
Dublin 13, Ireland

Text © Poolbeg Press Ltd 2016

A catalogue record for this book is available from the British Library.

ISBN 978 1 78199 876 2

Cover design and illustrations by Derry Dillon
Printed by GPS Colour Graphics Ltd, Alexander Road, Belfast BT6 9HP

This book belongs to

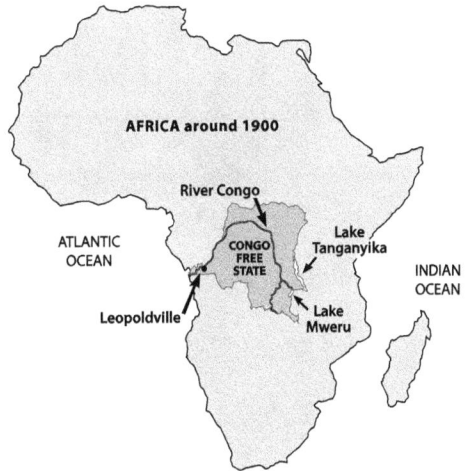

- -

Rathlin Island
Murlough Bay
ANTRIM
Belfast
ULSTER
CONNACHT
GALWAY
DUBLIN
Howth
Connemara
LEINSTER
Banna Strand
Ardfert
MUNSTER
Tralee Bay
WEXFORD
Tralee
CORK
KERRY
Cork City
Cork Harbour

COLOMBIA
ECUADOR
River Putumayo
River Amazon
PERÚ
BRAZIL

AFRICA around 1900

River Congo
SOUTH
PACIFIC
OCEAN
ATLANTIC
OCEAN
CONGO
FREE
STATE
Lake
Tanganyika
INDIAN
OCEAN
Leopoldville
Lake
Mweru

Available in the In a Nutshell Heroes Series

Pádraig Pearse and the Easter Rising 1916
Countess Markievicz — An Adventurous Life
James Connolly — Working Class Hero
Michael Collins — The Big Fellow

Adventure Calls

When Roger Casement was sixteen he had a job in the office of a shipping company in Liverpool, England. One day, he said to himself: 'I hate this! I must have an open-air life or I'll die!' So he got a job on one of the ships instead, carrying cargo back and forth to Africa. He was a purser, an officer taking care of the money and accounts.

Roger was Irish, born in Dublin in 1864, but he had been living in Liverpool with his aunt's family, the Bannisters. This was because, sadly, his mother died when he was only nine, and when he was twelve his father died too. After that, the four Casement children stayed with different relatives. In Liverpool, Roger and his little cousin Gertrude became close friends even though she was nine years younger than him. He wrote letters to her about his adventures for as long as he lived.

The Congo, Heart of Africa

When he was twenty Roger started to work in the Congo, for an organisation set up by Leopold II, King of Belgium.

The Congo was a huge country in the centre of Africa. It was covered in jungle, and the River Congo was thousands of miles long. The explorer Henry Stanley had followed the river from its source to its mouth. It took him 999 days – nearly three years!

After that, King Leopold hired Stanley to build a road, a railway and stations along the River Congo. Then Leopold claimed the whole of the Congo for himself. Not for his country, Belgium – just for him alone. He pretended he wanted to help the Africans develop their country but what he really wanted was to grab all the rubber, ebony and timber, and kill the elephants for ivory. Of course, he stayed safely in Belgium while his agents and private army ruled the Congo.

The trouble with the River Congo was that it had 200 miles of rapids, whirlpools and huge waterfalls thundering down with waves that could rip up giant trees. This is why, to get to the upper part of the Congo, Stanley's men had to build a road through the jungle and then a railway too. One of Roger's jobs was to plan the route of this railway.

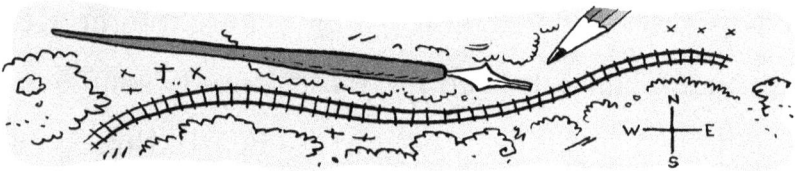

Of course, Roger knew nothing of Leopold's wicked plans. He got on with his work, walking hundreds of miles through the jungle, with a boy carrying the luggage on his head, and two bulldogs, Paddy and Biddy, bounding along with them. Later on, he got another dog too, a fox terrier called Spindle. One day its stomach was torn open by a wild boar. Roger was in shock but his friends pushed Spindle's guts back inside his stomach and sewed him up with needle and thread! He survived!

In Africa at that time lots of white people died of fevers like malaria from mosquitos. Roger did get malaria and it kept coming back all his life. He was often very sick, but he was tough and didn't die.

Then, back in Ireland in 1887, a man called John Dunlop made the first ever air-filled rubber tyre – for his son's tricycle! The modern bicycle had just been invented and Dunlop's tyres were perfect for a smooth ride. Suddenly everybody needed rubber and Leopold became a very rich man!

Soon after, Roger learned the horrible truth about the Congo. The Africans were being forced to tap rubber for Leopold. 'Tapping' meant they cut the

rubber trees or vines so that the sap dripped out into bowls. After that they boiled it until it set, cut it up and carried it in baskets to the agents' bases. But, if a village didn't make enough rubber, the agents' men sometimes killed them all, cut off their right hands and then brought baskets of hands back to their bosses to count. Or they would make the villagers lie down on their stomachs and flog them with whips made of hippopotamus hide. And sometimes they cut off their hands or feet. Even the children.

After that, Roger stopped working for Leopold's organisation and worked for a missionary instead. Then he went home to Ireland.

Her Majesty the Queen's Counsel

A few years later, in 1892, Roger was back in Africa, this time reporting on the River Niger for the British government. They were so impressed with him that they made him a British Consul. This meant he would be sent to live in foreign countries to protect other British people living there. Of course, at that time Ireland was ruled by Britain so Roger was considered to be British.

Roger had become a very important man!

Roger worked in several African countries and then, in 1903, he was sent back to the Congo. But first he was invited to lunch by King Leopold in Belgium! Roger told him about the terrible things happening in the Congo but Leopold denied everything.

Roger then made two trips to the Congo to investigate. On his way out the second time, a friend gave him a black bulldog called John. This dog was a demon but Roger adored him. When they arrived in the Congo, John had a fever and Roger was afraid he would die in the jungle so he arranged to send him back on a ship. But John took over the captain's cabin and wouldn't let the captain in! The captain had to send for Roger to remove him. So John got to go up the River Congo instead. He created havoc all the way, fighting with other dogs and chasing pigs and goats. Once, when they were visiting a village, he grabbed a goat by its leg and Roger had to choke him off in a headlock to save the goat.

Up the river, Roger discovered that the people were starving because they had no time to grow food. They had to spend all their time tapping rubber. Many fled far into the jungle to escape the agents. There they often starved or were eaten by leopards, crocodiles or cannibals.

Roger wrote everything down in his 'work' diary. He had a private diary too for his own personal stuff.

He also took photos of children with their hands cut off. One was of a boy called Epondo.

Finally, Roger felt he had enough evidence.

Back in England, his report on the Congo was published. But Leopold said that the people there were dying of a disease called 'sleeping sickness' and that Epondo's hand was bitten off by a wild boar.

Then Roger helped his friend Edmund Morel to form the Congo Reform Association, the first international human rights movement. They demanded that the Belgian government should take the Congo from their king and take care of it properly themselves. At last Leopold was forced to agree.

South America

In 1909, Roger was sent to Putumayo in Peru, South America. A rubber company called PAC was doing terrible things to the Indians there. These Indians were native people who had been conquered by the Spanish and the Portuguese centuries before.

PAC was also being cruel to black workers hired from Barbados in the Caribbean to control the Indians. Barbados was owned by Britain, so it was Britain's job to protect those workers.

Roger was sent with some important men to investigate. They travelled by ship up the Amazon through Brazil until they reached Peru. Then they travelled up the River Putumayo and met up with Juan Tizon, the chief agent of PAC. He had brought Indians to carry their luggage and Roger was shocked to see Barbadians too with whips to drive them along. Some of the Indians had wide scars on their backs and bottoms from being flogged.

The Barbadians later told Roger that they were forced by the agents to flog the Indians, who sometimes would even die from the flogging.

Here in Peru the Indians pressed the rubber into big flat sheets and rolled them up. They then tied some rolls together and carried them on their backs for huge distances to the agents' bases. Each person's load was weighed and if it wasn't enough the person would be flogged, even the children. The Indians were never paid anything for their work. Worse, they were hardly fed – just sometimes given a handful of cassava flour. They had no time to grow food for themselves so they were all starving.

When Roger confronted Tizon about all this, he confessed and promised that he would change everything.

Roger and the others then walked through the rainforest to a place called Entre Rios and on to a base where the boss, Normand, was an absolute monster. He was a thin man with the most horrible cruel face. He had forced many of the Indians' young daughters to live with him as his wives.

Disgusted, Roger set out to walk back to Entre Rios. There was a line of Indians carrying rubber down the path at the same time and he caught up with a woman carrying a huge load of rubber. She was crying and groaning, trembling all over. Then she fell to the ground. Roger took the load off her back but she called out over and over that Normand would kill her. Roger cried to see the state of her. He helped her to a hut on the road. She was naked like most of the Indian women so he dressed her in one of his pyjamas, lay her on his sleeping bag, put a warm coat over her and tried to feed her. She cried all night while he lay awake, with his revolver loaded, because he was afraid Normand or another vicious agent called Negretti would come and hurt the woman.

Negretti arrived next morning, driving forty women and children, shouting 'Hiti, hiti!' at them, meaning 'Go on, go on!' He was a thin dark man with teeth like a wild animal and glaring eyes. But Roger guarded the woman.

After Negretti left, Roger went on, leaving a Barbadian to take care of the sick woman and some others who had also collapsed.

Later Normand caught up with Roger and begged him not to report anything bad about him because he was always kind and gentle to the Indians! Roger ignored him.

At one village where Roger slept, a dog called Ladybird kept following him and went with him when he left. One night, at another village, he saw a lunar rainbow, a huge arc of light in the night sky. It was so awesome it cheered him up. Also, one early morning he took all the local dogs with Ladybird for a mad run up a hill! He got soaked because he was in his pyjamas and slippers and the high grass was wet with dew. That run really cheered him up!

He then met a little boy called Omarino carrying rubber and an older boy called Ricudo Arédomi. Roger weighed Omarino and his rubber and found that the rubber weighed more than the boy! He decided to take both boys back to London with him to let them tell their story.

Sir Roger Casement

Back in England in 1911 Roger was knighted at St James's Palace by King George V, for his wonderful work. He was now Sir Roger Casement. He didn't want the knighthood but it was good publicity for the Putumayo.

Omarino and Ricudo Arédomi were painted by a famous artist and met many important people. Later Roger took them back to Peru and found them jobs in the house of the British consul there.

When Roger's report on Putumayo was published everybody was shocked. After that things improved there. The evil agents ran away and Tizon kept his word and did his best to make things better for the Indians. Also, Roger arranged for some Franciscan missionaries to go there to take care of the people.

Back Home 1913

Roger had always been proud of being Irish. As a boy he had a little attic study where he stuck up pictures of Irish patriots who had been imprisoned by the English. On his home leave in 1904 he had helped organise the first Feis na nGleann (Festival of the Glens) in County Antrim, with Irish games, dancing and music. He loved the bagpipes!

Back home again in 1913, Roger heard that the poor people of Connemara in the West of Ireland were dying of a disease called typhus. He went there and persuaded rich people to give money for food and medicine. He got his friend William Cadbury, whose family made Cadburys' chocolate, to give free cocoa to the school there. Soon children from all over were queuing up for bread and cocoa. This was an Irish-speaking area and the only thing Roger asked of the school was that they should continue to speak Irish in the classroom and say the prayers in Irish. Roger loved the Irish language though he could only speak a little.

By this time Roger was completely against one country taking over another. It was time for him to help to free Ireland from Britain. He met the Irish Volunteers, who were training to fight for Irish freedom, and he masterminded a plan to buy rifles for them in Germany and have them landed by yacht in Howth near Dublin.

Then, in 1914, World War I began. Many thousands of Irishmen fought in the British Army against the Germans in Europe. Others felt they shouldn't fight for Britain.

Meanwhile, in Ulster, in the north of Ireland, many Protestant people didn't want to be free from Britain. Roger was upset by this. Ulster was his favourite place. His father was an Ulster Protestant but his mother was a Catholic from the south who secretly had her children baptised as Catholics when they were small. So Roger felt he belonged to both north and south and both religions.

Help from Britain's Enemy

Roger then went to America to talk to Irish people there who wanted Ireland to be free. They paid for him to go to Germany to get help for Ireland. A young Norwegian man called Adler Christensen, who spoke German, went with Roger. They travelled through Norway and there Adler went to the British and, for money, betrayed everything Roger was doing. Afterwards he told Roger that he had been questioned but that he didn't tell the British anything. Roger believed him. But now Roger knew the British were shadowing him.

In Germany Roger went to prison camps where British soldiers captured in the war were kept. There were 2200 Irishmen among them. Roger asked them to form an Irish Brigade to fight against the English. Only 50 of them agreed. This was a terrible disappointment for Roger.

Then, in early 1916, the Germans got a telegram from the Irish in America saying that there was going to be a Rising in Ireland at Easter, and the Irish Volunteers needed 100,000 rifles.

But the Germans sent only 20,000 rifles in a steamer they had disguised to look like a Norwegian ship called the *Aud*. Roger and two other Irishmen went in a submarine. They would meet the *Aud* in Tralee Bay on the west coast of Ireland. On the way Roger shaved off his beard, leaving only a moustache, so that he would not be recognised.

Roger felt the Rising was doomed. There were not enough arms and it was all being done in a rush. As it turned out, he was right.

Ten days later the submarine arrived at the time arranged, at midnight, but there was no *Aud* to meet them. Roger and the other two Irishmen tried to land in a small boat, but it overturned and they had to swim ashore to Banna Strand.

Arrest

They made their way to an ancient ring-fort, a place where the fairies lived according to the local people. Roger was very sick with fever so he stayed there while the others went to contact the Irish Volunteers. But, as he lay there listening to the skylarks high in the sky, the police suddenly appeared. Some of the local people had spotted Roger and his friends. Thinking they might be German spies, they called the police.

Roger was taken in handcuffs to Ardfert village. He didn't tell them his name and no-one knew who he was. He was taken to Tralee where the Chief Constable was very kind to him, cooking him a steak and drying his soaking clothes. Next morning, he was taken by rail to Dublin, then to England where he was put in the Tower of London. There he took some poison the Germans had given him. He wanted to die in case he might betray the Rising. But he did not die.

Later Roger heard that the Rising had failed and that the leaders were executed by firing squad. The *Aud* had been chased and captured by the British navy. Her crew had scuttled her and she sank in Cork Harbour with all the guns on board – but the crew were saved.

Roger's dear cousin Gertrude and her sister were on holiday by the sea. When they heard the awful news they rushed to London. They weren't allowed to see Roger for ten days. Then they visited him in a filthy cell, his skin all bitten with lice and bedbugs, no belt in his trousers or laces in his boots for fear he would try to hang himself with them.

High Treason

Roger was charged with high treason, which meant that he had betrayed England. His trial lasted four days. A friend had sent some of Roger's clothes to the prison and Gertrude later said he looked tall and noble as he stood in the dock.

Finally the jury returned with the verdict: Guilty!

The judge then delivered the awful sentence that Roger should be hanged by the neck until dead. He was to be hanged like a criminal instead of being shot like the other Easter Rising leaders.

After that Roger made a powerful speech to the court. He asked how he could be accused of high treason when he was an Irishman, not an Englishman, and his loyalty was to his own country – Ireland. He said that freedom is our right like the right to life itself.

Many people said that it was the greatest speech ever made.

He was moved to Pentonville prison and his knighthood was taken from him. His execution was set for the 3rd of August. At least, before he died he knew that most of the Irish people now wanted freedom, angry that the leaders of the Rising were shot and he was to be hanged.

Gertrude and many important people wrote letters and petitions to the British government, begging that his life be spared. But it was no use. Even worse, the government read his private diaries and discovered that Roger was gay. This was something he always had to keep secret because it was a crime to have a gay relationship at that time. The British showed those parts of the diaries to people who were trying to help him, and it turned many of them against him. That's the way people thought at that time.

On Gertrude's last visit Roger begged her to have him buried at Murlough Bay in Country Antrim in Ulster, a beautiful place by the sea that he loved. They cried together and then she had to go.

When she left the prison she wanted to shriek and beat on the gate with her hands, calling "Let him out! Let him out!" She staggered down the road, crying out loud, and people stared at her. Her heart was broken.

Last Sunset

The evening before the execution Roger stood in a little flower garden in the prison and watched the sun set for the last time.

When the morning arrived he received Holy Communion from a Catholic priest, though he had been a Protestant all his life. The priest went with him to the scaffold. He later said that Roger walked there with the dignity of a prince.

Then Roger was hanged.

Ellis, the hangman, said he was the bravest man he had ever executed.

Afterwards Roger was buried in the prison in quicklime to make his body rot more quickly.

A Hero's Welcome Home

But, as the great poet WB Yeats wrote,

The ghost of Roger Casement

Is beating on the door,

and the Irish people didn't forget his wish to be buried in Ireland. Nor did they give up the fight for freedom.

Ireland became a Free State and then a republic and the Irish government kept asking for his body to be returned home. The British government always refused.

Finally, nearly 50 years after his death, his bones were returned. They lay in a coffin in Arbour Hill, Dublin, and half a million people filed past to show their respect.

Then there was a state funeral. The coffin, draped in the Irish flag, was drawn in an army gun-carriage through Dublin to the sound of muffled drums. Thousands of silent people lined the streets. In Glasnevin cemetery, he was buried with full military honours with shots fired over his grave.

He would have preferred a simple funeral and a grave overlooking the sea in Antrim. But, no doubt, he would have been proud to see how the Irish people loved him and welcomed him home.

The End

GLOSSARY *(alphabetical order)*

association: a group of people joined together for a special purpose or common interest

bedbug: a small insect that is found in dirty bedding and feeds on human blood

brigade: a large group of soldiers that is part of an army

cargo: something carried from one place to another on a ship, plane or truck

cassava: an American plant whose roots can be eaten or made into flour

Catholic: a Christian who is member of the Roman Catholic Church

culture: the ideas, arts and customs of a particular people

dignity: calm, serious behaviour that makes people respect you

doomed: certain to fail, suffer or die

draped: covered loosely with a cloth

ebony: a hard black wood

firing squad: a group of soldiers that shoots a prisoner who has been sentenced to death

flog: to whip someone

folklore: traditional beliefs and stories

gay: 'gay' means 'light-hearted' but has come to mean a person who falls in love with people of the same sex as themselves

havoc: widespread destruction

headlock: holding someone firmly by putting an arm around the person's head

hide: the skin of an animal

international: belonging to many nations

investigating: trying to find out the facts about something

knight: in the Middle Ages a man who served his lord as a mounted soldier in armour. Now, a man given a title by the king or queen of England for some achievement.

knighthood: the state of being a knight

lice: small insects that live on the skin or in the hair of people and animals. One is called a 'louse'.

lunar: of the moon

mouth of a river: where it reaches the sea

muffled: not loud because the sound is blocked in some way, for example when drums are wrapped to dull the sound

organisation: a group of people who work together for a special purpose

passionate: having strong feelings

patriot: a person who has a strong love for his or her country

petition: a letter signed by many people, begging or demanding something

Protestant: a member of the Christian Churches that are not Catholic

quicklime: a chemical made from burning limestone rock or seashells

rapids: a fast-flowing rough part of a river where there is a steep slope

republic: a country where the power is held by the people and the government they elect

revival: re-awakening or bringing back into use

route: a way taken or planned

sap: the liquid in a plant

scaffold: a raised wooden platform used for the execution of criminals

scuttle: to deliberately sink a ship by putting holes in its sides or bottom

source of a river: where it begins

state funeral: a funeral organised by a government

vine: a plant with a very long stem that grows along the ground or up trees or walls

Some Things to Talk About

1. What parts of the book did you like most?
2. Did parts of the story upset you?
3. Do you think Roger enjoyed his life?
4. Would you like to have a life like Roger's?
5. Would you like to travel to see the Congo now? Or the Putumayo? Why or why not?
6. What did you think of King Leopold?
7. Why were the agents so cruel, do you think?
8. Do you think the Barbadians in Putumayo were wicked people?
9. Do you think the boys from Peru would have liked to stay in London instead of going back home?
10. Was Roger right to go to the Germans for help, do you think?
11. Do you think the people of Banna did a bad thing when they called the police?
12. Why did the crew of the *Aud* scuttle the ship?
13. Do you think it was right to try Roger for high treason?
14. Do you think it was right to read his private diaries?
15. Why, do you think, did Gertrude love her cousin so much?
16. Why did the British government want to make sure that Roger was hanged?
17. Why did they take away his knighthood?
18. If Roger wasn't hanged, what would have happened to him?
19. Was Roger a brave man?
20. Why did the British government refuse to send Roger's bones home for so long, do you think?
21. Why did so many people come to Roger's funeral?
22. Do you think Roger would be upset that he wasn't buried in Antrim by the sea? Or would he just be proud of the grand funeral he had in Dublin?

Timeline

1800: The 19th Century begins

1837: Victoria crowned Queen of Great Britain and Ireland

1864: Roger born in Sandycove, Dublin

1865: Leopold II becomes King of Belgium

1884: Roger begins work for Leopold in the Congo

1885: Leopold becomes ruler of the Congo Free State

1887: John Dunlop invents the rubber bicycle tyre

1895: Roger becomes a British Consul

1900: The 20th Century begins

1901: Queen Victoria dies – son Edward VII becomes king

1903: Roger's Congo Report

1904: Congo Reform Association, first international human rights association

1908: Belgians take the Congo from Leopold: it becomes the Belgian Congo

1910: Roger goes to Putumayo, Peru

Edward VII dies – son George V becomes king

1911: Roger knighted by George V

1914: Howth Gun-running, Ireland

The Great War (World War I) begins

Roger goes to America to talk to Irish-Americans

Roger goes to Germany to seek help for Ireland

1916: Easter Rising, Ireland

Roger's trial in London

Roger hanged on 3rd August at Pentonville Prison

Roger's state funeral in Dublin

2000: The 21st Century begins

2016 3rd August: 100th anniversary of Roger's death

www.ingramcontent.com/pod-product-compliance
Lightning Source LLC
Chambersburg PA
CBHW071745020426
42331CB00008B/2188